The Way to School

Plan International UK

New Internationalist

You probably enjoy going to school.

Even if you have a bad day now and then, wouldn't you miss it if you could never go?

Did you know that lots and lots of kids around the world would love to go to school but can't?

Some are very poor and must work to help their families.

Philippines

Japan

Sometimes disasters such as earthquakes, tsunamis

and typhoons destroy schools.

But whenever possible, kids try to make their way to school.

Maybe like you, they walk, or ride, or take the bus.

But for many children, the way to school is not that easy.

It can be long and hard and even scary.

United States

Philippines

What if there was a river in your way? Would you bravely wade across…

Cambodia

paddle across…

Indonesia

float across…

Nepal

Nepal

Colombia

or fly across?

China

Sometimes the only way to school is around a mountain…

or over a high cliff!

China

China

China

China

In many places, animals take children to school.
A donkey is perfect if the way is high and rocky.

An ox can pull a cartful of friends.

A water buffalo will take its time.

A dog team is useful
when you are in a rush,
and there is no road!

When there is no drinking water at school, some children must carry their own. A basin of water is much heavier than books!

Ghana

Uganda

Would you be willing to take your own desk to school?
If there was nothing to sit on, you might.

When rains come and waters rise, a temporary bridge can get you there. This one is low and quite safe.

Indonesia

This bridge was high once, but now it has collapsed and is very dangerous. These children use it to and from school each day.

Philippines

Sometimes a single wire becomes a bridge…

and sometimes a few bamboo poles must do.

Whether your way to school
is long and lonely,

Tanzania

Haiti

short and friendly,

Philippines

wide and wet,

Laos

narrow and dry,

India

or rugged and cold and slippery and high…

Haiti

…what matters is that you get there.
It's always worth the journey!

The Way to School

Published in 2016 by
New Internationalist Publications Ltd
The Old Music Hall
106-108 Cowley Road
Oxford OX4 1JE, UK
newint.org

First published by Second Story Press, Toronto, Canada
secondstorypress.ca

© Plan International Canada
Text by Plan International Canada with Rosemary McCarney.

British Library Cataloguing-in-Publication Data
A catalogue record for this book is available from the British Library.

ISBN 978-1-78026-343-4

Photo Credits

Cover: (front) Saikat Mojumder/Plan (back) Mark Foster, Asti Alanna De Guzman, Mikko Toivonen/Plan
Page 3: Mardy Halcon/Plan
Page 4: Richard Jones/Sinopix
Page 5: Jane Rivera/Plan
Page 7: © iStock/Purdue9394
Page 8: Asti Alanna De Guzman
Page 9: Mark Foster
Page 10: Iggoy el Fitra
Page 11: (top left) David Sowerwine/ Village Tech Solutions, (top right) Tyler Miller/Village Tech Solutions, (bottom) Fanny Gauret/Learning World Euronews
Page 12: HAP/Quirky China News/REX
Page 13: HAP/Quirky China News/REX
Page 14: (left) HAP/Quirky China News/REX, (right) HAP/Quirky China News/REX
Page 15: HAP/Quirky China News/REX
Page 16: MM/Color China Photo/Sipa
Page 17: Wen Leonardo/Sipa Press
Page 18: Andrey
Page 19: DEDDEDA
Page 20: Nyani Quarmyne/Plan

Page 21: Mikko Toivonen/Plan
Page 22: Quirky China News/REX
Page 23: Iggoy el Fitra
Page 24: Asti Alanna De Guzman
Page 25: Iggoy el Fitra
Page 26: James Stone/Plan
Page 27: Rose-Carmille Jeudy/Plan
Page 28: Asti Alanna De Guzman
Page 29: Jim Holmes/Plan
Page 30/31: Timothy Allen
Page 32: Ben Depp/Plan